For: Jaxon

D0668197

DEVOTIONAL
MINUTES
FOR BOYS

Jean Fischer

DEVOTIONAL MINUTES FOR BOYS

Inspiration
from
God's Word

BARBOUR **kidz**

A Division of Barbour Publishing

Published Barbour Publishing, Inc., 1810 Barbour Drive, Uhrichsville, Ohio 44683, www.barbourbooks.com

Our mission is to inspire the world with the life-changing message of the Bible.

Member of the
Evangelical Christian
Publishers Association

Printed in The United States of America.

001059 0122 SP

INTRODUCTION

There is a special time for everything.
ECCLESIASTES 3:1

One minute. That's all it takes to read each story in this book. Each minute will teach you about God, the Bible, and some of its special and most interesting people. You might even learn a little about *you*! The Bible says there is a time for everything. So set aside one minute each day to spend here with God. Better yet, spend that minute with a parent reading this book together.

• •

Dear God, I can't wait to see
what is inside. Let's go! Amen.

5

JOSIAH, THE BOY-KING

*Josiah was eight years old
when he became king.*
2 CHRONICLES 34:1

The Bible is filled with stories that teach us about God and people who loved and obeyed Him. Josiah was just eight years old when he became king of a place called Judah. He decided to be brave and trust God to help him. Josiah learned from God, and he did great things as Judah's king. You can do great things too—whatever you do—if you trust in God for help.

•••••••••••••••••••••••••••••••••••

Dear God, I will trust You to help me. Amen.

GOD IS

And God said to Moses, "I AM WHO I AM."
EXODUS 3:14

God has always existed. He will exist forever. It's impossible to understand everything about God because He is so great—greater than anything your human brain can understand. God sent a man named Moses to talk with some people. Moses wondered who he should say sent him. God answered, "Say, I AM sent you." God is the great I AM. He is bigger and better than anyone or anything. He *is* and He *always* will be.

• •

Dear God, I want to learn more about You. Amen.

CREATOR!

*In the beginning God made from nothing
the heavens and the earth.*

GENESIS 1:1

God made the whole universe in just six days! He created light, the sky, land, oceans, plants, trees, the sun, the moon, and stars. He made animals that live in water, birds that fly, and animals that live on land. Then God made a man and a woman, Adam and Eve. People are God's greatest creation. God made them "in His image." This means God is the best example of how He wants people to live.

● ●

I would like to become more like You, God. Amen.

FOREVER

For You made the parts inside me.
You put me together inside my mother.
PSALM 139:13

God made you, and He made you just the way He wants you to be. He knows all about you. God even knows your future. You can't know yet what God has planned for you. As you get older, He will reveal those secrets to you. You can always trust God to guide you. He won't leave you—ever! When He made you, God planned for the two of you to be together forever.

• •

Dear God, it's You and me together forever! Amen.

GOOD PLANS

*" 'For I know the plans I have for you,' says
the Lord, 'plans for well-being and not for
trouble, to give you a future and a hope.' "*
JEREMIAH 29:11

God's plans for you are good. Allow Him to lead you.
Follow God and obey Him, and He will help you stay out of
trouble. Do you wonder what plans He has for you? What
would you like to do when you grow up? God might lead
you there, or maybe He has something even better waiting for you.

● ●

*Dear God, I trust that Your plans
for me are good. Amen.*

MOSES

"I know that You can do all things.
Nothing can put a stop to Your plans."
JOB 42:2

God had great plans for Moses. But Moses was afraid. He didn't speak well. He didn't want to stand up to important men and say the words God wanted Him to say. But nothing stops God's plans. God gave Moses a helper to speak his words, and God gave Moses courage. Moses became a great leader—one of the greatest in the Bible.

• •

Dear God, when I think I can't do something,
give me helpers and the courage to try. Amen.

JESUS

Jesus is the Christ, the Son of God.
JOHN 20:31

God sent His Son, Jesus, to earth as our Helper. First, Jesus was a baby, then a young boy like you. Jesus was different though, perfect like His Father, God. He taught people the right ways to live. He grew up to be the greatest teacher of all. Jesus is alive and with us today. You can't see Him, but you can believe He is with you and helping you.

• •

Dear Jesus, I can't see You with my eyes,
but I can feel You in my heart. Amen.

FOREVER LIFE

*"Whoever puts his trust in God's Son will not
be lost but will have life that lasts forever."*
JOHN 3:16

Jesus allowed Himself to be nailed to a cross, and all the world's sins—the bad things people do—for all time were poured into His heart. He did that so you can live with Him forever in heaven someday. Jesus took the punishment for the bad things you do, so you never have to worry that God won't forgive you if you mess up. Jesus loves you!

• •

Jesus, thank You. I love You too. Amen.

GOD UNDERSTANDS ME

"Is He not a Man Who makes things from wood?"
MARK 6:3

Jesus' dad, Joseph, made things from wood. He taught Jesus to make things from wood too. Maybe your dad teaches you things. Jesus learned many skills from His dad here on earth. In that way, Jesus was a lot like you when He was growing up. Although He was perfect and God's Son, Jesus knew what it was like to be human. That's one reason He understands you so well.

●●

*Dear Jesus, however I'm feeling, whatever
I do, I know You understand. Amen.*

GOD KNOWS

God is greater than our heart. He knows everything.
1 JOHN 3:20

You can find the answers to most things if you search hard enough. God doesn't have to look for answers, because He already knows everything. He doesn't have to study or learn. God knows answers to questions like "What is beyond the stars?", "Where is heaven?", and "Why do zebras have stripes?" God is all-knowing, and He knows all about you. No one and no thing is greater than God.

• •

Dear God, because You know me
so well, I can feel special. Amen.

EVERYWHERE

The eyes of the Lord are in every place,
watching the bad and the good.
PROVERBS 15:3

God can see everything going on in the world. He sees you all the time all at the same time. That might make you feel like God is spying on you, but instead He is watching over you. God made you. You are one of His kids, and He keeps His eyes on you because He loves you. God is with you all the time. You can always call on Him for help.

● ●

Dear God, I'm glad You are always with me. Amen.

JONAH

"Can a man hide himself in secret places
so that I cannot see him?" says the Lord.

JEREMIAH 23:24

A man named Jonah decided not to obey God. Instead, he ran away, boarded a ship, and was thrown overboard. A big fish swallowed Jonah. He was in its belly for three days. God saw Jonah. He was with Jonah all the time. When Jonah asked God for help, the big fish spit Jonah out. Jonah had learned that wherever you go, you can't hide from God.

• •

God, I will do my best never to hide from You. Amen.

SUPERPOWERS

"For God can do all things."
LUKE 1:37

Who is your favorite superhero character? It's fun to pretend that make-believe characters have amazing powers. But God is the *only* One with *real* superpowers. The Bible says that God turned Aaron's walking stick into a snake. God led an army to knock down the walls of an evil city just by playing one long note on their trumpets. God made the sun stand still. The Bible is filled with true stories about things God did. He can do *anything*!

• •

Dear God, no one has superpowers like Yours. Amen.

MIRACLES

"What kind of a man is He? Even the winds and the waves obey Him."

MATTHEW 8:27

Jesus is the Son of God! He can do all kinds of superpower things like His Father does. When He lived on earth, Jesus healed people from many sicknesses. He even brought some who were dead back to life. He told a big storm to stop, and it did. Jesus did many amazing miracles. The people said, "What kind of man is this? Even the winds and the waves obey him!" (Matthew 8:27 NIV).

● ●

Jesus, I want to know more about You. Amen.

WALKING ON WATER

*Just before the light of day, Jesus went
to them walking on the water.*
MATTHEW 14:25

You can swim in water, and ski and surf on water. You can't walk on water. But Jesus did! His followers—His disciples—were on the water in a small boat. It was nighttime, and dark and windy. The boat was being tossed around by the waves. Then they saw Him. Jesus was walking toward them on the water. Who else do you know who can walk on water but the true Son of God?

● ●

Jesus, You are amazing! Amen.

MEGA-LUNCH

"There is a boy here who has five loaves of barley bread and two small fish. What is that for so many people?"
JOHN 6:9

A huge crowd listened to Jesus speak. Hours passed. They were hungry. The disciples hadn't planned for a big lunch. But Jesus knew what to do. He asked a boy to share his five small loaves of bread and two fish. Amazingly, Jesus made that lunch grow and grow until everyone in the crowd was fed. Jesus always gives us what we need.

• •

Jesus, You know what I need even before I ask. Amen.

FISHING FOR MEN

"Follow Me. I will make you fish for men!"
MATTHEW 4:19

Some of Jesus' disciples were fishermen. Jesus told them, "Follow Me. I will make you fish for men!" What did He mean? Jesus meant that He would teach His disciples to become more like Him. Then they would teach others how to follow Jesus. Those people would teach more people and on and on—until the whole world would know about Jesus. You can be a disciple too. Learn all you can about Jesus. Then teach others to follow Him.

• •

Jesus, I want to follow You. Amen.

I CAN DO IT

I can do all things because Christ gives me the strength.
PHILIPPIANS 4:13

Jesus Christ lives in your heart. You can't see Him, but He's in there. He's the One who helps you to be brave when the doctor gives you a shot or when you are the new kid in school and you don't know anybody. Jesus can make you strong to face all the hard stuff. He's right there with you all the time. You can talk with Him just by saying a prayer.

• •

Thank You, Jesus, for making me strong. Amen.

PRAYING

Hear my prayer, O God. Listen to the words of my mouth.
PSALM 54:2

Talk with God. He hears you every time you pray. You can tell Him anything. If you are feeling a little ashamed about something you said or did, you can tell God about it. He already knows what happened, and He forgives you. One of the best things about prayer is that you can tell God things you might not be ready to tell others. You can trust God to listen and show you what you should do.

● ●

Here I am, God. Let's talk. Amen.

QUIET PRAYER

Never stop praying.
1 THESSALONIANS 5:17

When you pray, you don't have to speak your words. You can think your prayers, and God will still hear them. All the time you can talk with God just like you would with a parent or a friend. God wants to hear from you. He's interested in everything you do. You can ask Him for help if you need it. You can talk with Him if you're lonely. You can talk as much as you want! God likes hearing your voice.

* * *

Dear God, let's talk together all day long. Amen.

LISTEN

Long ago God spoke to our early fathers in many different ways. He spoke through the early preachers.
HEBREWS 1:1

Do you know that God speaks to us? He speaks through that little voice in your head that guides you to do what is right. God speaks to us through His Son, Jesus, too. When you read Jesus' words in the Bible, it is like God speaking to you. When you pray, take time to listen. You just might hear God's voice speaking to you in your head.

• •

*Dear God, I will be quiet sometimes
and listen for Your voice. Amen.*

JESUS KNOWS

*Jesus knew what they were thinking. He said to
them, "Why do you think this way in your hearts?"*
LUKE 5:22

If you knew people's thoughts, that would be a superpower!
Jesus knows all of our thoughts. He always knows what
people are thinking. Don't let that worry you. Everyone
has bad thoughts sometimes. Understanding that Jesus
knows our thoughts helps us to want to behave better so
our thoughts will please Him.

* *

*Dear Jesus, even before I pray, You know
my thoughts and are working to help and
provide me with what I need. Amen.*

BEHEMOTH!

*"He is the first of the works of God.
Let his maker bring him his sword."*
JOB 40:19

God created every animal, and cares for and has control over each one, no matter how large. Perhaps one of the biggest was the powerful behemoth. It hid in the tall river grass and was said to have a tail like a cedar tree. Its bones were strong like iron. How do you imagine behemoth? What's the biggest animal you have seen?

• •

*Dear God, I love learning about Your animals.
Thank You for making them. Amen.*

ALL-POWERFUL GOD

"I am the Lord, the God of all flesh.
Is anything too hard for Me?"
JEREMIAH 32:27

Nothing gets in God's way. Not even the biggest things, like the mighty behemoth, the tallest mountains, or the biggest waves in the oceans. Why? Because God made them all. He has power over everything. Nothing is too hard or Him to do. God is the Master of the universe, so if something big gets in your way, ask Him for help. God is on your side. He will always help you.

• •

All-powerful God, You keep me safe. Amen.

GOD POWER!

*But the people of Israel walked
on dry land through the sea.*
EXODUS 14:29

Moses led God's people, the Israelites, away from an evil
pharaoh. Pharaoh's army followed the Israelites! When
the Israelites came to the sea, they thought they were
trapped. God told Moses to put his hand out toward the
water. When Moses did, God parted the sea! The Israelites
walked through on dry land. The sea was like walls on either
side of them. Whenever we face trouble, God's power kicks
in. He is our Helper.

•••

Dear God, I trust in Your power. Amen.

LITTLE THINGS

"God knows how many hairs you have on your head."
LUKE 12:7

Some of the tiniest things mentioned in the Bible are insects like fleas and ants, and you can imagine tiny ocean creatures like ghost shrimp, miniature snails, and floating worms. God made them. He knows every detail about every little thing. He even knows how many hairs are on your head right now. And if one hair comes out on your comb, God knows that too. Nothing is too small for God to care about.

• •

*God, You know everything about
me, even the tiniest things. Amen.*

ONE STAR, TWO STARS, THREE STARS. . .

He knows the number of the stars.
He gives names to all of them.
PSALM 147:4

Guess how many stars there are? Scientists think there are more than one hundred billion stars in the Milky Way alone! And who knows how many more there are far beyond what we can see? God knows. He made all the stars. He knows exactly how many there are, and He has names for each one. If a meteor—a "shooting star"—falls to earth, God knows that too.

• •

Dear God, You know everything! Amen.

TALENTS

We all have different gifts that God has given to us.
ROMANS 12:6

When you grow up, would you like to be a star athlete—maybe a football, basketball, or baseball player? To become a star, you have to become really good at what you do. God gives us different talents—things we are good at. You might not be good at sports, but you are good at something else. Work hard at your special talents. Who knows? Someday what you are good at might make you a star.

• •

Thank You, God, for my special talents. Amen.

GIVE IT YOUR BEST

*Whatever your hand finds to do,
do it with all your strength.*
ECCLESIASTES 9:10

Whether you are good at something or not, whatever you do, give it your best. Nobody can be perfect, but everyone can work hard. If you try to become better at doing something, God sees you trying. When you try and do your best, it pleases Him. If it's homework, cleaning your room, learning to kick a soccer ball, or something else, do it with all your strength.

• •

*Dear God, I will work hard because
I want to please You. Amen.*

DON'T GIVE UP

"Be strong and do not give up,
for your work will be rewarded."
2 CHRONICLES 15:7 NIV

In the Bible, a man named Daniel kept working at what he knew was right even when others wanted him to do what was wrong. It wasn't easy, but Daniel kept doing what he knew was good and pleasing to God. That's what you should do too. Always do your best to do what is right, and don't give in to what you know is wrong.

• •

Dear God, I won't give up doing what I know is right. Amen.

DANIEL

*The king said to Daniel, "May your God,
Whom you are faithful to serve, save you."*
DANIEL 6:16

The Bible tells this true story: when Daniel wouldn't give up on God and do the evil things the king wanted, the king threw Daniel into a den of hungry lions and locked the door. God protected Daniel. He sent an angel to shut the lions' mouths. God knew Daniel hadn't done anything wrong, and He kept Daniel safe. When you do what is right, you can always trust God to protect you.

• •

Thank You, God, for keeping me safe. Amen.

WINNER, WINNER

*You know that only one person gets a crown
for being in a race even if many people run.
You must run so you will win the crown.*

1 CORINTHIANS 9:24

It feels good to win, doesn't it? Winning means you tried hard and it paid off. But always remember that God is the One who helped you win. He gave you what you needed to win, whether it was something you learned to do well or the physical strength to play your best. Give Him your thanks.

• •

Dear God, thank You for helping me win. Amen.

SO COOL

*"The person who thinks he is important
will find out how little he is worth."*
MATTHEW 23:12

Some people, when they do something great, act all cool and say, "Look at me!" Jesus said we should be humble—which means knowing that what you did was amazing and being proud of what you did, but not telling the world how wonderful you are. When you're humble, you set a good example for others.

• •

*Dear God, when I accomplish something great,
I want to tell someone! When I talk about
me, please help me to be humble. Amen.*

I'M A GOOD SPORT

Therefore encourage one another and build each other up.
1 THESSALONIANS 5:11 NIV

If someone else wins the game, do you say, "Good job"? That's being a good sport. The Bible says we should build others up to help them feel good about themselves. If you are the winner, being a good sport also means encouraging others by saying something nice like, "You played well. Maybe next time you'll win." Think about it: are you a good sport?

Dear God, whether I win or lose,
remind me to be a good sport. Amen.

TEAMWORK

Two are better than one, because they
have good pay for their work.
ECCLESIASTES 4:9

Watch any team sport, and you'll see people working together for one reason: they want to win the game. Teamwork is important, not just in sports but in everything. When people work together, they can get things done quicker and usually better. Teamwork takes getting along well with others, listening to ideas, and sharing. Can you think of a time when you worked together with others to get something done?

• •

God, I know teamwork is good because
it brings people together. Amen.

DARKNESS

From noon until three o'clock it was dark over all the land.

MARK 15:33

While Jesus hung on the cross dying, the sky turned dark. His followers cried. They didn't know what they would do without Him, their Friend and Teacher. Most people weren't sure yet that Jesus was God's Son. That's why their leaders nailed Jesus to the cross. They thought He lied about being the Son of God. But Jesus was about to do something awesome. He was going to live again!

• •

Dear Jesus, I'm sad they thought You lied. You always tell the truth. Amen.

SUNLIGHT

"He is not here! He has risen from the dead."
MATTHEW 28:6

A man named Joseph buried Jesus' body inside his own new tomb and rolled a big stone in front of its door. It seemed like Jesus was gone forever. But three days later, in the early morning, Jesus' followers found the stone rolled away. An angel was there. His face lit up like the brightest sunlight! "Are you looking for Jesus?" he asked. "He is not here! He has risen from the dead." The tomb was empty. Jesus' body was gone!

• •

Dear Jesus, I am so thankful that You rose from the dead. Because You live forever, I can too. Amen.

ALIVE!

A cloud carried Him away.
ACTS 1:9

Jesus was alive. People saw and talked with Him. But then, as His followers watched, Jesus went back to heaven to be with His Father, God. He was lifted up on a cloud! He went up and up until they couldn't see Him anymore. Angels came and said, "This same Jesus Who was taken from you into heaven will return" (Acts 1:11). Jesus is still with us in His Spirit. But one day He will come back—body and all.

• •

Jesus, You are alive in my heart. Amen.

HEAVEN

"I am going away to make a place for you."
JOHN 14:2

Jesus has made a place for you to live in heaven someday. You get to heaven by admitting you sometimes do bad things, asking God for forgiveness, and believing that Jesus loves you so much that He already took the punishment for all the bad things you'll ever do. God doesn't have favorites. Heaven is for everybody. It's a special, perfect, and happy place where people can live with Him forever.

● ●

*Jesus, thank You for loving me and
saving a place for me in heaven. Amen.*

BACK AGAIN

*"You heard Me say that I am going
away. But I am coming back to you."*
JOHN 14:28

You can't see Jesus, but He has the superpower to be with you always even though He's invisible. Jesus said that one day He will show up on earth again in His body. He will come back to get rid of all the bad stuff happening on earth. Until then, we know Jesus is with us as our Helper, loving us and watching over us.

• •

I love You, Jesus. I'm glad You are always with me. Amen.

TEAM JESUS

"Go and make followers of all the nations."
MATTHEW 28:19

Just before Jesus left the earth and went up to heaven,
He told His followers, "Teach [others] to do all the things I
have told you" (Matthew 28:20). So His followers formed
a team. They worked together for one reason: to teach the
whole world about Jesus. Look around and you will see Team
Jesus at work even today. Every person who tells someone
about Jesus is a member of His team.

• •

*Dear Jesus, I'm joining Your team! I want
to tell others all about You. Amen.*

BEAUTIFUL FEET

"The feet of those who bring the Good News are beautiful."
ROMANS 10:15

The Bible books Matthew, Mark, Luke, and John are called the "Good News." They tell Jesus' story from the day He was born. Jesus wants us to share His story. In Bible times, people got around by walking. Some walked for miles and miles just to share the story of Jesus' life. Maybe that's why the Bible says, "The feet of those who bring the Good News are beautiful."

• •

Jesus, I will learn the story of Your
life and share the Good News. Amen.

SCALY-EYED SAUL

"Saul, Saul, why are you working so hard against Me?"
ACTS 9:4

Saul hated Jesus' followers. He tried stopping them from sharing the Good News. A bright heavenly light appeared, and Saul heard Jesus' voice: "Why are you working so hard against Me?" Then Saul couldn't see. Something scaly covered his eyes. Jesus sent Saul to a man who put his hands on Saul's eyes, and the scales fell away. He could see again! Now Saul believed in Jesus. He promised to follow Jesus forever.

•••

*Dear Jesus, I want to love Your people and
always do things that please You. Amen.*

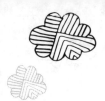

SAUL OR PAUL?

I, Paul, am one of Christ's missionaries.
COLOSSIANS 1:23

Saul had two names: his Hebrew name, Saul, and a Roman name, Paul. Sometime after he began following Jesus, he used his Roman name. If you read the New Testament in the Bible, you'll see Paul's name often. He became one of the best-ever Jesus followers and teachers. Paul wrote thirteen books of the Bible. He had plenty to say about how God wants us to live. Read his words and learn from him.

● ●

Dear God, thank You for teachers like Paul. Amen.

SHIPWRECK!

"I believe my God will do what He has told me."
ACTS 27:25

Some people hated Jesus' followers. More than once, Paul was put in prison for sharing the Good News. He was held prisoner on a ship when the ship met a terrible storm. God's angel told Paul the ship would sink but all the people on board would live. Paul had faith in God. He told the captain what the angel said. The ship did sink, but everyone was saved. God's words are always true. Paul knew that and believed. Read more about Paul's shipwreck in Acts 27.

• •

God, I trust Your words. Amen.

FAITH

It is good to hear that your faith is so strong in Christ.
COLOSSIANS 2:5

Faith is believing that everything about God is true. Faith is trusting in Jesus' words and God's promises no matter what. Paul never lost his faith, not even when he was in prison or when it seemed everyone turned against him. He stayed close to God. Especially in hard times, Paul never stopped believing. How strong is your faith? Would you keep believing in God even when things didn't go your way?

• •

Dear God, help me to have a strong faith like Paul's. Amen.

SAVED!

"Put your trust in the Lord Jesus Christ."
ACTS 16:31

Paul was chained in prison when an earthquake happened. Everything shook. His cell opened and his chains fell off, but he didn't run away. The prison guard was terrified. "What must I do to be saved?" he cried (Acts 16:30). Paul told the man about Jesus, and the man put his trust in Him. God did a miracle that day. He saved Paul from prison, and He saved the guard from a lifetime of sin.

• •

Dear Jesus, I will help others to find faith in You. Amen.

LETTERS

"His letters are strong and they make us think."
2 CORINTHIANS 10:10

Paul was locked up in prison. Still, he shared the Good News. He wrote letters to his friends, telling them about Jesus and the things He taught. In Paul's time, there were no phones or computers. Everyone wrote letters. Today we send texts. We can even see each other when we talk on our phones. Can you think of a few different ways you could share the Good News about Jesus?

● ●

Dear Jesus, show me how to share the Good News. Amen.

LOVE

Those who do not love do not know God because God is love.
1 JOHN 4:8

In his letters, Paul wrote about love. He said love is patient and kind. It's not jealous. Love is being humble. Love does what is right. It's unselfish. It doesn't get angry, and it forgives. Love hates what is bad and loves what is true. Love doesn't give up. It believes in and hopes for the best. Love keeps going on. It never ends. The Bible says that God is love. He loves with a love that is perfect.

• •

Dear God, teach me Your kind of love. Amen.

PATIENCE

*But if we hope for something we do not
yet see, we must learn how to wait for it.*

ROMANS 8:25

"Just wait!" Waiting is hard, and even harder when you're hoping for something. Whether it's a gift, doing an activity you enjoy, or going to a favorite place, you want it right away. Paul wrote about patience. It means waiting without getting upset. If anyone was patient, it was Paul. He trusted that when the time was just right, God would give him what he hoped for and exactly what he needed.

• •

Dear God, help me to be more patient. Amen.

KINDNESS

*"Those who show loving-kindness are happy, because
they will have loving-kindness shown to them."*
MATTHEW 5:7

The Bible tells the true story of a man who was robbed,
beaten, and left lying in the road. Three men passed by.
Two saw the man lying there, but they didn't help. Only
one man stopped. He cared for the man and brought him
to a safe place. He was kind. He cared about others a lot.
Jesus said, "Those who show loving-kindness are happy."
Why do you think they are happy?

* *

Dear Jesus, please teach me more about kindness. Amen.

MANY KINDS OF KINDNESS

You must be kind to each other.
EPHESIANS 4:32

Kindness is shown in many different ways. You show kindness to your parents when you help around the house and show kindness to your brothers and sisters when you share your toys. Kindness is saying nice things to people and doing little things that make their lives easier. It's little unexpected surprises and thinking about other people's feelings. Can you think of even more ways to treat others with kindness?

• •

Dear God, please give me ideas for ways
I can show kindness to others. Amen.

JOSEPH

"The sons of Jacob sold Joseph to people from the country of Egypt because they were jealous of him."
ACTS 7:9

The Bible says Joseph's brothers were jealous of him because they thought he was their dad's favorite. So they did something mean. They sold Joseph to be a slave. Things worked out okay for Joseph, though. He became an important man in Egypt. As mean as they were to him, Joseph forgave his brothers. He forgave them, because in his heart he knew it was right.

• •

Dear God, I hope I can be as forgiving as Joseph. Amen.

JEALOUSY

*Wherever you find jealousy and
fighting, there will be trouble.*

JAMES 3:16

Jealousy is when you feel unhappy or angry because someone has something you want. Everyone feels jealous sometimes, even grown-ups. There are ways to turn around that unhappy feeling. Paul said love isn't jealous, so you could think of what you love about the person you're jealous of. You can also think of things you are thankful for. Best of all, you can pray and ask God to help with your jealous feelings.

• •

*Dear God, when I feel jealous, help
me to turn that feeling around. Amen.*

FORGIVE THEM

*Jesus said, "Father, forgive them. They
do not know what they are doing."*
LUKE 23:34

People were mean to Jesus. They hurt Him badly. But when Jesus was dying on the cross, He said to God, "Father, forgive them. They don't know what they are doing." You can remember Jesus' words when people hurt your feelings and make you feel sad. Jesus understands how you feel. You can talk with Him about it and ask Him to help you forgive.

•••

*Dear Jesus, someone hurt my feelings. I know You
understand. Will You help me to forgive them? Amen.*

61

HOW MANY TIMES?

"I tell you, not seven times but seventy times seven!"
MATTHEW 18:22

How much is seventy times seven? If you aren't sure, ask someone. Four hundred ninety is a lot, isn't it? But that's how many times Jesus said we should forgive those who hurt us. He didn't mean that we should keep allowing people to hurt us. He meant that if we don't feel like forgiving someone, we should keep trying to forgive them in our hearts. Forgiving someone helps us feel less angry or sad.

• •

Dear Jesus, even when it's hard,
I'll keep trying to forgive. Amen.

GRRRRRRRR!

If you are angry. . .get over your
anger before the day is finished.
EPHESIANS 4:26

Go ahead, do it—roar like an angry lion! We all have days when anger creeps in. It makes us want to shout and say mean words. If we were lions, we would all roar: *Grrrrrrrr!* But we're not lions. The Bible says we should get rid of our anger before each day is done. So don't fall asleep feeling angry.

● ●

Dear God, angry roars are for lions but not for me. Amen.

MY TURN!

An unfriendly person pursues selfish
ends and. . .starts quarrels.
PROVERBS 18:1 NIV

Paul said that love isn't selfish. Imagine you are ready to bat a ball. Your friend grabs the bat out of your hands and says, "My turn!" If your friend had acted with God's kind of love, he would have let you take your turn before taking his. The Bible teaches that selfishness starts quarrels. What would you have said to your friend when he tried to take your turn?

•••••••••••••••••••••••••••••••••••••••

Dear God, I don't want to start fights. Will you
help me handle unfairness Your way? Amen.

HOPE

And now, Lord, what do I wait for? My hope is in You.
PSALM 39:7

Paul said that love believes in and hopes for the best. What do you hope for? Hope isn't only about wanting something for yourself. It's also about hoping for and wanting the best for others. You show love for others when you hope for good things for them. God can do anything. Whatever you hope for, when you put your hope in Him, He promises to provide what is best.

• •

Dear God, I will try harder to put my hope in You. Amen.

WHAT IF—?

"Not what I want, but what You want."
LUKE 22:42

Jesus asked God to save Him from dying on the cross. But He added, "Not what I want, but what You want." Even if Jesus didn't get what He wanted, He trusted God to do what was best. If you don't get what you want, you might feel sad. But Jesus understood—and you can too—that God's plans for you are even better than what you hope for.

● ●

*Dear God, even if I don't get what I
want, I won't stop trusting You. Amen.*

TELL THE TRUTH

*"He that is not honest with little things
is not honest with big things."*
LUKE 16:10

"Did you eat another piece of candy?" Mom asked. Little brother said, "No!" But he did eat the candy. It was a tiny lie, so he thought it didn't matter. All lies, both little and big, are wrong. Jesus said someone who tells little lies will probably tell big lies too. When you tell the truth, you will please God, your parents, and others. And that's a good thing!

• •

*Dear God, telling the truth is important.
Thanks for reminding me. Amen.*

DO WHAT'S RIGHT

*My son, if sinners try to lead you
into sin, do not go with them.*
PROVERBS 1:10

Your friend wants you to play with him inside his dad's
backyard toolshed. You know that your friend's dad told
him to stay out of there. What should you do? Giving in and
doing what you know is wrong is never a good idea. The
Bible warns against it. Saying no and walking away takes
courage. But it's the right thing to do.

• •

*Dear God, give me courage to say no
to doing things that are wrong. Amen.*

WHAT IS A SIN?

The person who keeps on sinning is guilty
of not obeying the Law of God.
1 JOHN 3:4

What is a sin? A sin is anything that displeases God. If you love God, you want to obey Him and follow His rules. Nobody is perfect. Everyone sins. But because God loves you, He sent Jesus to take the blame for your sins. When you sin, if you've put your trust in Jesus, you can be sure that God forgives you.

• •

Dear God, I don't want to displease You. But
thank You for forgiving me when I do. Amen.

GOD'S GUIDEBOOK

[The Bible] shows what is wrong. . .
[and] how to be right with God.
2 TIMOTHY 3:16

If you went hiking on a new trail, you might have a guidebook to follow. It would tell you the right way to go and even places you shouldn't go. The Bible is God's guidebook. It teaches us what God says is right and wrong. As you read and study the Bible, you will learn about who God is and how to follow the right path through life.

••

Dear God, I will read my Bible, and You will teach me. Amen.

MOSES AGAIN

Moses was a faithful servant.
HEBREWS 3:5

You will see Moses' name many times in the Old Testament. From the day he was born until he died, Moses made news. (Read about baby Moses in Exodus 2:1–10.) God chose Moses to lead His people, the Israelites, to a new land God had saved just for them. Along the way, God gave Moses stone tablets on which God wrote ten important rules we all should follow. They are called the Ten Commandments.

•••

Dear God, I want to know more about Your ten rules. Amen.

RULE ONE

"Have no gods other than Me."
EXODUS 20:3

God's first rule is that we have no gods other than Him.
God is the One and only God. He wants to be more important than anything or anyone else in our lives. When Jesus
was asked which of God's laws was most important, He
answered, " 'You must love the Lord your God with all
your heart and with all your soul and with all your mind.'
This is the first and greatest of the Laws" (Matthew
22:37–38).

•••

Dear God, I want You always to come first in my life. Amen.

RULE TWO

"Do not make for yourselves a god to look like anything that is in heaven above or on the earth below or in the waters under the earth."

EXODUS 20:4

While Moses was away getting the stone tablets with God's rules, the Israelites made a statue of a calf out of gold. They bowed down to it and worshipped it like a god. This made God angry. Statues and other objects have no power and shouldn't be worshipped. God is all-powerful and the only One who should be prayed to and praised.

• •

Dear God, I will worship only You. Amen.

RULE THREE

"Do not use the name of the Lord your God in a false way."
EXODUS 20:7

Words are important to God. His third rule says He wants us to respect His name. Not only His name but the names of His Son, Jesus, and the Holy Spirit. Have you heard people use God's or Jesus' names in disrespectful ways? Doing this is wrong. And never lie using their names. The names *God* and *Jesus* should always be used in good and respectful ways.

• •

Dear God, I will respect Your and Jesus' names. Amen.

74

RULE FOUR

"Remember the Day of Rest, to keep it holy."
EXODUS 20:8

God said we should make the seventh day of the week a day of rest. He explained why: "In six days the Lord made the heavens, the earth, the sea and all that is in them. And He rested on the seventh day. So the Lord gave honor to the Day of Rest and made it holy" (Exodus 20:11). Most Christians set aside Sunday as a special day of rest to worship and honor God.

• •

Dear God, on Sunday and every day I will honor You. Amen.

RULE FIVE

"Honor your father and your mother."
EXODUS 20:12

What does it mean to honor your father and mother? In part, it means remembering that God gave you parents to help you grow up. It's their job to teach you. Your parents set rules they believe will lead you to live the right way. God's fifth commandment is just for you. You should respect and obey your parents, not only because you love them but because that's what God wants you to do.

• •

Dear God, I will try even harder to
honor and respect my parents. Amen.

RULE SIX

"Do not kill other people."
EXODUS 20:13

Even long ago when God gave Moses the Ten Commandments, people got angry and killed one another. Killing is always wrong. When Jesus said, " 'You must love the Lord your God with all your heart and with all your soul and with all your mind.' This is the first and greatest of the Laws," He added, "The second [Law] is like it, 'You must love your neighbor as you love yourself' " (Matthew 22:37–39).

● ●

*Dear God, I pray that people will stop getting
so angry that they kill one another. Amen.*

RULE SEVEN

"Be faithful in marriage."
EXODUS 20:14 CEV

Maybe someday you will get married. God says that when people marry, they become one person. That means the one you marry will be closer to you than any other human on earth. To be faithful in marriage means putting your wife first before anyone else except God. It means giving her all your love and respect and working together as a team in everything you do.

• •

Dear God, if I get married someday, I will be sure to remember Your rule number seven. Amen.

RULE EIGHT

"Do not steal."
EXODUS 20:15

God's eighth rule says, "Do not steal." The Bible tells about a man named Micah, who stole his mother's silver. He used it to make a statue of a god that he could bow to and worship. Micah broke three of God's rules. Can you guess which ones? He stole something, he made and bowed in worship to a false god, and he broke God's first rule: "Have no gods other than Me."

••

Dear God, it was wrong for Micah to steal. Help me not to break Your rules like he did. Amen.

RULE NINE

"Do not tell a lie about your neighbor."
EXODUS 20:16

Rule number nine is about lying. Think about this: How would you feel if someone told a lie about you? Your feelings would be hurt, wouldn't they? You might even feel angry. Lying about someone is hurtful to them. Lying is hurtful to God too. He hates lies. So if you feel a lie about to leave your lips, stop it and tell the truth instead.

•••••••••••••••••••••••••••••••••••••••

Dear God, lying leads to trouble. It is best to follow Your ninth rule and always tell the truth. Amen.

THE TENTH COMMANDMENT

"Do not want anything that belongs to someone else."
EXODUS 20:17 CEV

The last rule on God's stone tablets is about jealousy—wanting what others have. God is good to His children, and that's who *you* are—God's child! God made you. He is your heavenly Father, and He promises to give you everything you need. He might not always give you what you want, and when He doesn't, it's because He knows best. If you feel jealous sometimes, God understands. He will forgive you.

• •

Dear God, please forgive me for
wanting what others have. Amen.

A SPECIAL BOX

"Put into the special box the Law which I will give you."
EXODUS 25:16

God told Moses to build a special box called an "ark" for the stone tablets. Moses put the tablets inside. When the Israelites continued their journey to the land God had waiting for them, they carried God's rules in the box with them. You can carry God's rules with you too by keeping the Ten Commandments inside your heart so you will remember them all the time.

• •

Dear God, I will memorize Your Ten
Commandments so I won't forget them. Amen.

NOAH

But Noah found favor in the eyes of the Lord.
GENESIS 6:8

Noah's ark wasn't like the box that held the Ten Commandments. His "ark" was a kind of boat. It was huge, and it held two of every kind of animal on earth. God was displeased with the way people were behaving, so He planned a do-over to right the wrong things happening on the earth. If you started going the wrong way, God would allow you a do-over too.

● ●

Dear God, when I misbehave, You will always give me another chance to do what is right. Thank You! Amen.

A BIG BOAT

Make it four hundred fifty feet long, seventy-
five feet wide, and forty-five feet high.
GENESIS 6:15 CEV

When God makes something, He often does it big. Mountains, oceans, the universe—God made them all. He gave Noah plans for building the big boat. Noah made it from wood, and there were rooms inside for the animals. When it was finished, the ark was longer than a football field, almost as wide as two Brachiosauruses lying nose to nose on the ground, and about as tall as a four-story building!

• •

Dear God, Your plans are always
perfect and wonderful. Amen.

A BIG FLOOD

The flood came upon the earth.
GENESIS 7:17

God told Noah and his family to get on board the ark and take with them two of every kind of animal on earth. Noah obeyed God. All were on board and ready. Then God made it rain. A great flood covered the whole world. The water was so deep it even covered the mountains! God's do-over had begun. But Noah's family and the animals were safe in the ark floating atop the water.

• •

Dear God, I know that whatever
happens, I am safe with You. Amen.

A YEAR IN THE ARK

And the water covered the earth for 150 days.
GENESIS 7:24

It rained for 40 days. Everything on earth washed away. For 150 days, the earth was totally covered with water. Then, one day, the water started going down. God's do-over was finished. Noah and his family waited patiently for the flood to end. It was more than one year before Noah and the others left the ark. The earth was washed clean of sin and ready to start again with Noah's family and the animals.

• •

Dear God, I want patience like Noah's. Amen.

A PROMISE

"There will never again be a flood to destroy the earth."
GENESIS 9:11

Noah praised God for His goodness. Then God made a forever promise. He said there will never again be a flood to destroy the earth. God set a rainbow in the sky as a symbol of His promise. Whenever you see a rainbow, remember Noah's story. God's promise to Noah is one of many promises God makes in the Bible. When He promises something, God always follows through. His promises last forever.

•••

Dear God, all of Your promises are right and good. Amen.

A FAITHFUL FATHER

God is faithful.
1 CORINTHIANS 1:9

God is faithful. What do you think that means? A faithful person is someone you can depend on. You can always depend on God for everything. A faithful person makes a promise and does his best to keep it. God always keeps His promises—every one. God never goes back on His word. When He says something, you can trust that it's true. God promises to be a faithful Father to you forever.

• •

Dear God, You are my faithful heavenly
Father. I can always depend on You. Amen.

GOD'S PERFECT LOVE

Give thanks to the God of heaven. His love endures forever.
PSALM 136:26 NIV

"I love you to the moon and back." If someone says that to you, it means that person loves you with a lasting love that's big. God's love for you is even bigger. Every day God keeps pouring His love into your heart, and His love never runs out. God loves you all the way past the moon, through the stars, into the universe, and all the way to heaven. God promises to love you forever.

●●●●●●●●●●●●●●●●●●●●●●●●●●●●●●●●●●●

Dear God, I love You too. Amen.

BAD NEWS, GOOD NEWS

The Lord is good, a safe place in times of trouble.
NAHUM 1:7

People were behaving badly, doing evil things. So God sent a good man named Nahum to give them a message. The bad news was that God was going to punish them. The good news was that those who loved and obeyed God would be safe from God's punishment. God promises to keep safe those who trust Him. When you put your trust in God, nothing can stand in your way.

• •

Dear God, You have power over trouble,
and I feel safe with You. Amen.

I'M NEVER ALONE

"The Lord is the One Who goes before you. He will be with you. He will be faithful to you and will not leave you alone. Do not be afraid or troubled."

DEUTERONOMY 31:8

God promises never to leave you. God is everywhere. He knows what is coming before you do. You can trust that He's always with you. Even if you don't feel God around you, He's there. Remembering that will help calm you down at times when you feel afraid.

• •

Dear God, I will remember today's Bible verse to help me when I'm scared. Amen.

COMFORT

*He is our Father Who shows us loving-kindness
and our God Who gives us comfort.*
2 CORINTHIANS 1:3

God promises to comfort you when things aren't going well. You can trust in His love all the time. Comforting means helping others to feel better when they have trouble. If you're sick, your mom might comfort you by wrapping you in a warm blanket and cuddling with you while you watch a movie together. God often brings us helpers to comfort us when things go wrong.

• •

*Dear God, I feel Your love in my
heart, and it comforts me. Amen.*

JESUS, MY HELPER

*But Jesus took him by the hand
and helped him and he stood up.*

MARK 9:27

When you read about Jesus in the Bible, you will see Him
helping others with His actions and words. Jesus promises
to be your Helper too. If you need help, close your eyes, say
a prayer, and imagine Jesus right there with you. He's with
you all the time, ready to help with all your needs. What
do you need help with today?

* *

*Dear Jesus, I need a little help today. Let's spend
some time together and talk about it. Amen.*

HELP EACH OTHER

*Remember to do good and help each
other. Gifts like this please God.*
HEBREWS 13:16

The Bible says, "If someone has the gift of speaking words of
comfort and help, he should speak. If someone has the gift
of sharing what he has, he should give from a willing heart.
If someone has the gift of leading other people, he should
lead them. If someone has the gift of showing kindness to
others, he should be happy as he does it" (Romans 12:8).

• •

*Dear God, tell me: Which of my
gifts can I share today? Amen.*

DIFFERENT GIFTS

*There are different kinds of gifts. But it
is the same Holy Spirit Who gives them.*
1 CORINTHIANS 12:4

God gives us different kinds of "helping gifts"—the special ways we help each other. Some people have the gift of a strong body and are good at lifting and carrying things. Others have the gift of lifting spirits. To lift someone's spirit means to help them feel better when things go wrong. Can you think of helpers in your community who help in different ways?

● ●

Dear God, how can I use my gifts to help others? Amen.

GOD'S CHILDREN

God does not see you as a Jew or as a Greek. . . . He does not see you as a man or as a woman. You are all one in Christ.

GALATIANS 3:28

God made us to be different, but we are alike in the best possible way—we are His. We are all God's children, and He loves us just as we are. Think about your friends. In what ways are you different? In what ways are you alike?

● ●

Dear God, You don't have favorites. We are all Your children, and You love us the same. Amen.

EVERYONE IS BEAUTIFUL

I praise you because of the wonderful way you created me.
PSALM 139:14 CEV

When God made you, He made you one of a kind. Everyone is one of a kind; no two people are alike. God made people to look different from one another—different skin, eyes, hair, and so on. And everyone is beautiful in God's eyes. When God looks at you, He thinks you are His boy—His perfect, handsome boy. And He loves you.

Dear God, thank You for making us one of a kind and members of Your big, beautiful family. Amen.

BROTHERS AND SISTERS

Love each other as Christian brothers.
Show respect for each other.
ROMANS 12:10

Jesus said, "This is what I tell you to do: Love each other"
(John 15:17). We should love others like they were our
brothers and sisters. God made us all. Every person in the
world is His. God is our heavenly Father, and that makes us
one big family. We will be a happy family if we do our best
to get along and love each other.

• •

Dear God, I will do my best to love everyone
as if they were my sisters and brothers. Amen.

I HAVE POWER

Show other Christians how to live by your life.
1 TIMOTHY 4:12

When you think of something powerful, you might think of something big. But size doesn't matter when it comes to teaching others about God. You might be little, but you have power! You have power to set a good example for others by the words you say and the things you do. You also have power to teach others about Jesus and why it's important to become more like Him.

• •

Dear God, I'm young, but I can do mighty things. Amen.

JUST SAY NO!

Every child of God has power over the sins of the world.
1 JOHN 5:4

If a little voice in your heart leads you to sin—to do something you know is wrong—you have power over that voice. Just tell it, "No!" That one word gives you the power to do what is right. And if that little voice in your heart is loud and you really, *really* want to do what is wrong, you can have faith that Jesus will help you. Just ask Him.

• •

Dear Jesus, please help me to say no. Amen.

BUT I'M AFRAID

*"Do not be afraid or lose faith. For the Lord
your God is with you anywhere you go."*
JOSHUA 1:9

Do you feel afraid sometimes? Everyone does. But God gives you power over fear. God has power over everything. You already know that He is always with you and He loves you. So when you feel afraid, you can pray and ask Him to make you strong. If you remember that God is right there with you, it will help you feel less afraid.

• •

Dear God, I need Your power to make me strong. Amen.

BRAVE BOY

"You are not able to go and fight against this Philistine. You are only a young man."
1 SAMUEL 17:33

God's army, the Israelites, fought an evil group of soldiers called the Philistines. One of the Philistine soldiers, Goliath, was big and strong and almost twice as tall as most men. When the Israelite soldiers saw him, they ran away from him, afraid. But a brave young shepherd boy named David wasn't afraid to fight Goliath. David knew God was on his side.

Dear God, I know You are on my side. Amen.

STRONG BOY

He gives strength to the weak. And He gives
power to him who has little strength.
ISAIAH 40:29

Goliath was a warrior who was more than nine feet tall. He
wore a bronze helmet, a heavy bronze coat of scale armor,
and bronze leg coverings. He carried a huge bronze spear on
his back. A man walked before him to carry his shield. Still,
young David wasn't afraid to fight Goliath. He trusted God
to make him strong, and God gave him the skill and power
to defeat the giant Goliath.

● ●

Dear God, when I face trouble,
You will give me strength. Amen.

ALL THAT I NEED

"You come to me with a sword and spears.
But I come to you in the name of the Lord."
1 SAMUEL 17:45

David took five stones and his sling—a weapon for shooting stones—and ran toward Goliath. The giant laughed and made fun of him. David put one stone in his sling and fired. It hit Goliath on the forehead, and down he fell. David didn't need battle clothes or military weapons. God gave him everything he needed to fight his enemy.

• •

Dear God, You give me all that I need. Amen.

PAUL AGAIN

Put on the things God gives you to fight with.
EPHESIANS 6:11

Jesus' follower, Paul, faced many battles, but he learned not to fight with weapons. Instead, he fought with good things like truth; a heart that loved God; peace that came from knowing Jesus; faith that Jesus had saved him from sin; and trust in God's Word, the Bible. These things, Paul said, are like invisible armor—protective clothing that people can put on to fight against evil.

Dear God, I want armor like Paul's. Amen.

BELT OF TRUTH

Wear a belt of truth around your body.
EPHESIANS 6:14

Truth is important. Without it people won't trust you. If you always tell the truth, others will believe everything you say. Truth is the first part of God's armor. Like a belt that holds up your pants, the belt of truth holds your armor together. God's soldiers need to be truthful in all they say and do, and it's important for them to know the truth of God's Word.

•••

*Dear God, each morning I will put on my belt
of truth and wear it all day long. Amen.*

BREASTPLATE OF RIGHTEOUSNESS

Wear a piece of iron over your chest.
EPHESIANS 6:14

Armor includes a metal plate worn across your chest. Its purpose is to protect your heart. The Bible calls this piece of armor the breastplate of righteousness. God lives inside your heart. That's why it's important to allow only good things inside. A good heart loves God and does what pleases Him. When you always try to do what is right, this piece of armor stays strong.

• •

Dear God, I will protect my heart by doing what I know is right. Amen.

SHOES OF PEACE

Wear shoes on your feet which are the Good News of peace.
EPHESIANS 6:15

If you walked over rocks barefoot, you would get cuts, bruises, and blisters on your feet. Good, solid shoes are another part of God's armor. They help you to walk a difficult path. Paul said you should wear shoes that bring the Good News of peace. Wherever your feet take you, bring with you peace and the Good News about Jesus' love.

. . . .

Dear God, I will do my best to bring peace into the world and tell others about Jesus' love. Amen.

SHIELD OF FAITH

Most important of all, you need a
covering of faith in front of you.
EPHESIANS 6:16

Faith means believing that everything about God is true. It is trusting in Jesus' words and God's promises no matter what. Paul said you should carry a shield of faith to protect you from anything that tries to get in the way of you believing in and trusting God. A shield is the most important part of your armor.

• •

Dear God, I won't let anything get in the
way of the faith I have in You. Amen.

HELMET OF SALVATION

*The covering for your head is that you have
been saved from the punishment of sin.*
EPHESIANS 6:17

Soldiers in God's army wear helmets to protect their heads.
The Bible says you are to put on the helmet of salvation.
You wear it to remind you that Jesus saved you from sin.
When He died on the cross, Jesus took the punishment for
all the bad things people do. We deserved that punishment,
but Jesus took it instead. Protect that information. Keep
it safe inside your brain.

•••

*Dear Jesus, thank You for taking
the punishment I deserved. Amen.*

SWORD OF THE SPIRIT

Take the sword of the Spirit which is the Word of God.
EPHESIANS 6:17

Paul called the Word of God the "sword of the Spirit." The Bible is filled with verses you can use for help whenever you need it. Trouble is like that big soldier, Goliath, in David's story. Bible verses are like David's stones—they can knock trouble down. Memorize Bible verses so you will have them ready when you need them. Can you say any from memory?

• •

Dear God, I will try to memorize at least one Bible verse each day. Amen.

FOLLOW THE LEADER

The Lord went before them.
EXODUS 13:21

When Moses led the Israelite army away from the evil pharaoh, God went ahead of them. Like an army general, God led the way. What does God look like? Nobody knows. He was in a thick cloud when He led the Israelites in daytime and in a flaming fire when He led them at night. Wherever you go, remember that although you can't see God He always leads the way.

• •

*Dear God, I can't see You, but I know You
are going ahead of me, leading me. Amen.*

BUGS!

*The God Who lives forever is the Lord,
the One Who made the ends of the earth.*
ISAIAH 40:28

When you explore the Bible, you'll discover all kinds of things God made, even creepy, crawly, and flying bugs. You could start your own bug collection by finding these Bible verses: Exodus 8:17, lice; Exodus 8:21, flies; Leviticus 11:22, locusts, crickets, and grasshoppers; Deuteronomy 7:20, hornets; Judges 14:8, bees; Proverbs 6:6, ants. God is the great Creator of everything!

•••

*Dear God, I like watching bugs!
I'm glad You made them. Amen.*

ADAM

*And whatever the man called a
living thing, that was its name.*
GENESIS 2:19

God made the first human, a man named Adam. God made
him from dust, and He put Adam in a beautiful, perfect
garden called Eden. God planted trees in the garden with
delicious fruit for Adam to eat. God put Adam in charge of
caring for the garden. He brought every living thing, every
animal, to Adam, and He allowed Adam to name them all.
Do you have a pet that you've named?

• •

*Dear God, thank You for making so many different
kinds of plants and animals for us to enjoy. Amen.*

ONE RULE

"But do not eat from the tree of learning of good and bad."
GENESIS 2:17

God created a partner for Adam, a woman named Eve. They lived in the garden, and they had just one rule. (Can you imagine? Just one!) Among the trees, there was the tree of learning of good and bad. *"Don't eat from that one,"* God warned. Adam and Eve knew only what was good. What do you think might happen if they ate from a tree that taught them both good and bad?

• •

Dear God, I will obey Your rules. Amen.

SNAKE!

And the woman said, "The snake fooled me, and I ate."
GENESIS 3:13

An evil snake came into the garden. It said, "When you eat from the forbidden tree, your eyes will be opened. You will be like God, knowing good and bad." *What's wrong with that?* Eve thought. So she and Adam ate the fruit. Then they saw not only what was good but also sin—the bad stuff. God was angry. He made Adam and Eve leave the garden. Because of sin, their lives weren't beautiful anymore.

• •

Dear God, I won't be fooled by sin. Amen.

GOOD FRUIT

"A tree is known by its fruit."
MATTHEW 12:33

Jesus said, "A tree is known by its fruit. A good tree gives good fruit. A bad tree gives bad fruit." He wanted people to think about their own behavior. A person who behaves well is like a tree that grows good and tasty fruit. A person who behaves badly is like a tree that grows rotten or bad-tasting fruit. How was your behavior today? What kind of tree were you?

* *

Dear God, I want my behavior to be like
good fruit, the kind everyone loves. Amen.

SPIRIT FRUIT

*"Every tree that does not have good fruit
is cut down and thrown into the fire."*
MATTHEW 7:19

When you belong to God, His Holy Spirit speaks to your conscience and leads you to choose good behavior over bad. Paul called good behaviors—like love, joy, peace, patience, kindness, goodness, faithfulness, gentleness, and self-control—the fruit of the Spirit. When we love God, we try to behave in good ways that please Him.

•••

*Dear God, thank You for Your Holy Spirit
who helps me to choose what is right. Amen.*

FRIENDS

A friend loves at all times.
PROVERBS 17:17

Think about today's Bible verse: "A friend loves at all times."
It's easy to love your friends when they behave well. But
what about times when a friend's behavior makes you angry
or sad? Friends don't always get along. When that happens,
think about your own behavior. Are you doing your best to
be a good friend? How do you think you could show some
love to a friend who is behaving badly?

Dear God, help me to love my friends,
even when it's hard. Amen.

JOY!

*Be full of joy always because you belong
to the Lord. Again I say, be full of joy!*

PHILIPPIANS 4:4

What is the most joyful time you can remember? Maybe it's
the day you got a new pet or the time your grandpa took
you fishing or on another adventure. God brings all kinds
of things into our lives that bring us joy. Just knowing how
good God is should fill our hearts with joy. If it weren't for
Him, we would have nothing to be happy about.

Dear God, thanks for all the joy You bring me. Amen.

DAVID AND JONATHAN

Those who plant seeds of peace will
gather what is right and good.
JAMES 3:18

In the Bible, David and Jonathan were best friends. Jonathan's dad, King Saul, didn't like David, and that was a problem. Jonathan knew that David was a good guy and worthy of being liked, so he talked with his dad and tried to get him to live in peace with David. Being a peacemaker is like planting a seed. If that seed takes root, it can grow into something beautiful.

• •

Dear God, please teach me to be a peacemaker. Amen.

KEEP GOING!

Do not let yourselves get tired of doing good. If we do not give up, we will get what is coming to us at the right time.

GALATIANS 6:9

Mateo went to ask his neighbors for canned goods to give to a local food bank, but his neighbors were either not home or busy. "I give up!" Mateo said. He didn't know that if he had kept going he would have collected a lot of food for the food bank. Never give up too easily. Trust in God's help.

● ●

Dear God, please help me not to give up. Amen.

PAY IT FORWARD

If you show loving-kindness, God will
show loving-kindness to you.
JAMES 2:13

If you have the flu, you do your best not to give it to someone else. You don't want the flu to spread around. But there is something that you should want to spread—kindness! Kindness is contagious—it's catchy. It's something you want to spread around. If someone thanks you for something kind you did, you can say, "Pay it forward." That means they should do something kind for someone else.

● ●

Dear God, it's good that kindness is contagious. Amen.

GOODNESS

"My people will be filled with My goodness," says the Lord.
JEREMIAH 31:14

What do you think "goodness" means? Did you say, "Behaving well"? Goodness is more than behaving well. Goodness is becoming like Jesus. He was good all the time. Jesus not only behaved well, but He did good work. Everywhere He went, Jesus helped people, and He led others to be helpers too. Ask Jesus to fill you up with His kind of goodness. Then you will be more like Him.

• •

Dear Jesus, I want Your kind of goodness
to fill up my heart. Amen.

FAITHFUL FRIENDS

"I will go where you go."
RUTH 1:16

The Bible tells about Ruth and Naomi. When Naomi was going through a really bad time, Ruth promised never to leave her. Friends stick together in good times and bad. Ruth was a faithful friend! Faithfulness means being loyal—being a true friend in good times and bad. God is that kind of friend. You can count on His faithfulness always. He says, "I will never leave you or let you be alone" (Hebrews 13:5).

● ●

*Dear God, thank You for being my
loyal and faithful Friend. Amen.*

GENTLENESS

Let all people see how gentle you are.
PHILIPPIANS 4:5

Anthony met his baby sister for the first time. She was so tiny! "Would you like to hold her?" Mom asked. "Be gentle." Anthony was very careful holding his sister. She was like a precious gift. He wanted to take good care of her. God wants all of us to treat each other the way Anthony treated his sister. We need to be gentle with our actions and words and careful to not hurt someone's feelings.

•••••••••••••••••••••••••••••••••••••

Dear God, give me a spirit that's gentle and kind. Amen.

WHO'S THE BOSS?

*Paul spoke about being right with God. He spoke
about being the boss over our own desires.*

ACTS 24:25

God is the boss of us all. He rules over the earth. But you are
the boss of your own mind. You can let good or bad thoughts
lead your mind. If you think about good things like love,
joy, peace, not giving up, kindness, goodness, faithfulness,
and gentleness, then your thoughts will be pleasing to God.

*Dear God, please help me to keep my mind
set on good thoughts that please You. Amen.*

HAPPY THOUGHTS

*If there is anything good and worth giving
thanks for, think about these things.*

PHILIPPIANS 4:8

If you were feeling unhappy right now, what could you think about that would make you feel better? Thoughts that turn unhappy thoughts to happy ones come from God. He gives us many good things to be thankful for. If you store up memories of all those good things, you can remember them whenever you feel sad. What are some of your happiest thoughts?

• •

*Dear God, thank You for reminding me of
all the good things You give me. Amen.*

I AM TRULY LOVED

Keep your minds thinking about whatever is true.
PHILIPPIANS 4:8

Oliver's mom saw he was having a bad day. "God loves you," she said. "Jesus loves you. I love you. Daddy loves you. So does Grandma and Grandpa, your brothers and sisters, your aunts, uncles, cousins. . ." The long list of people who loved Oliver cheered him up. When he thought about it, Oliver smiled because he knew it was true—he was loved.

● ●

Dear God, I made a list of people who love me. I am truly loved. Amen.

RESPECT

Keep your minds thinking about whatever is. . .respected.
PHILIPPIANS 4:8

Respect means thinking and caring about how your words and actions affect others. It also means being careful not to damage places or things. As you think about and work at being more respectful, you'll learn another kind of respect— respect for yourself. That means you will feel good about the kind of person you are becoming, one who cares about others and pleases God.

• •

Dear God, I will do my best to be respectful
of people, places, and things. Amen.

THAT'S RIGHT!

Keep your minds thinking about whatever is. . .right.
PHILIPPIANS 4:8

Mason entered his scout troop's pinewood derby. He was supposed to make his car from a kit that had wood, wheels, and nails. But instead of making a car, Mason took his older brother's car. It was fast and won the derby when his brother entered. The Bible says to think about whatever is right. Do you think Mason was right to take his brother's car instead of making his own?

• •

Dear God, I will think about and do what is right. Amen.

PURE THOUGHTS

Keep your minds thinking about whatever is. . .pure.
PHILIPPIANS 4:8

It's a steamy hot day. Your mom brings you a cup of ice-cold water. Just as you're about to put the cup to your lips, a big ugly stink bug falls into your drink. It's not pure anymore. It's ruined. The Bible reminds us to keep our thoughts on things that are pure—thoughts that have nothing ugly or stinky in them. How are your thoughts? Do you keep them pure?

Dear God, please help me to have pure thoughts. Amen.

I LOVE. . .

Keep your minds thinking about whatever. . .can be loved.
PHILIPPIANS 4:8

Think about this: What do you love to do? Name three things. Now name three things you love to eat. How about three things you love to look at? Name three kinds of animals you love. How about three people you love? When you fill up your brain with thoughts of what you love, you'll notice even more how lovely God's world is.

• •

Dear God, there are so many things
I love about Your world. Amen.

A SPECIAL BABY

Jesus said to them, "Yes, have you not read the writings,
'Even little children and babies will honor Him'?"
MATTHEW 21:16

Jesus came into the world the way you did, as a baby boy.
God had great plans for Him. Jesus would grow up to save
the world from sin. When Jesus grew into a man, even little
children knew how special He was. They honored Jesus with
praise, calling out to Him, "Greatest One! Son of David!"
(Matthew 21:15).

• •

Dear Jesus, thank You for coming to earth to be born
as a baby. Just as Your Father had great plans for You,
You have great plans for me. I praise You! Amen.

A SIMPLE BEGINNING

She put cloth around Him and laid
Him in a place where cattle are fed.
LUKE 2:7

Where were you born? In a hospital? At home? The Bible says Jesus was born in a place where cows were fed. He didn't have a cozy bed or doctors and nurses caring for Him. God planned for Jesus to have a very simple beginning. But this baby who was born in the simplest possible way would grow up to do the greatest thing of all.

• •

Dear God, You even make simple things great. Amen.

A SPECIAL NIGHT

"I bring you good news of great joy which is for all people."
LUKE 2:10

It was an ordinary night, but God was about to do something extraordinary. Shepherds were watching their sheep when an angel appeared in a bright, heavenly light. He told them that Jesus had been born. "There will be something special for you to see.... You will find the Baby with cloth around Him, lying in a place where cattle are fed" (Luke 2:12). Then the sky filled up with angels praising God.

••

Dear God, I wish I could have seen that! Amen.

DO YOU BELIEVE?

*When they saw the Child, they told
what the angel said about Him.*
LUKE 2:17

The angel told the shepherds that this baby, Jesus, was the One who would save the world from the punishment of sin. The shepherds went to see Him. They told everyone what the angel had said. All who heard it were surprised. Do you think they believed the shepherds' words? Jesus' mom, Mary, believed. She hid those words in her heart and thought about them much.

• •

*Dear Jesus, I believe! God sent You to save
us from the punishment of sin. Amen.*

THE STAR

*"We have seen His star in the East.
We have come to worship Him."*

MATTHEW 2:2

God set a bright star in the East. Wise men who studied the stars saw it. They believed that if they followed the star, they would find Jesus. They knew He was special. They believed that someday He would be a great leader of the Jewish people. But they didn't yet know how great Jesus would become. They followed the star and brought Jesus gifts fit for a king.

• •

*Dear Jesus, You were and are greater
than any earthly king! Amen.*

AN ANGRY KING

Herod. . .was very angry.

MATTHEW 2:16

On the way to find Jesus, the wise men met Herod, king of the Jews. They told him about the star and Jesus. Herod knew that long ago, men told of a Messiah—a special person God would send to save the world. Herod thought Jesus might be the One. That made Him jealous and angry. *He* was the greatest one, not Jesus! Herod wanted the boy killed. But God had a plan to save Jesus' life.

• •

Dear God, Your plans are always perfect. Amen.

THE GREAT ESCAPE

"Go as fast as you can!"
MATTHEW 2:13

An angel visited Joseph, Jesus' father on earth. He warned that Herod wanted to kill Jesus. So Joseph took his wife, Mary, and Jesus to a safe place. As fast as they could, they packed their things and moved to Egypt. They stayed there until King Herod died. Then God told Joseph to move his family again, and they went to a town called Nazareth.

• •

Jesus, You must understand how kids feel if their family has to move. Yours moved a lot! Amen.

SOMETHING NEW

"See, I will do a new thing."
ISAIAH 43:19

God often leads us toward something new. Maybe it's moving to a new town, like Jesus' family did, or a new school, or even a new activity. Life would be boring if you stayed in the same spot forever. Experiencing new things is part of growing up. If God leads you someplace new, you might feel a little nervous, but God knows where you should be. His plan for you is good.

● ●

Dear God, help me to feel less nervous when I try something new. Amen.

KING OF KINGS

He is the King of kings and Lord of lords.
1 TIMOTHY 6:15

Jesus grew up in the town called Nazareth, but then He moved on. He traveled around teaching people about God, showing them the right way to live. Everywhere He went, people followed, wanting to hear Him speak. They knew Jesus was special, but they didn't know yet who He really was. One day they would understand—Jesus is the Son of God, King of all kings, Lord of all lords, the world's Savior.

••••••••••••••••••••••••••••••••••••

Dear Jesus, I'm glad I know who You are. Amen.

AN EVIL PLAN

The proud religious law-keepers went
out and made plans against [Jesus].
MATTHEW 12:14

Do you remember King Herod, the one who wanted baby Jesus killed? Long after King Herod died, there were people who followed his ways. They hated the grown-up Jesus. They were jealous of all the followers Jesus had and how popular He was. So, just like Herod did, they made plans to kill Jesus. They didn't know yet that nothing could stop Jesus, *nothing* at all.

• •

Dear Jesus, You are all-powerful.
Nothing can get in Your way. Amen.

SATAN

Jesus said to the devil, "Get away, Satan."
MATTHEW 4:10

Herod's friends weren't the only ones who tried to stop Jesus. Satan, the devil, tried to stop Him too. For forty days and nights, Satan tried to get Jesus to do wrong things, but Jesus wouldn't. He went without food that whole time. He was hungry but didn't give in. "Get away, Satan!" He said. And, finally, Satan left. Angels came then and cared for Jesus.

• •

*Jesus, I want to be like You and not give in when
Satan wants me to do what is wrong. Amen.*

RUN AWAY

*So give yourselves to God. Stand against
the devil and he will run away from you.*
JAMES 4:7

Disobey your parents. It's okay. Satan, the devil, puts ideas
in your head to try to get you to do wrong. He also came
to Jesus and tried to stop Him from going to the cross to
die for our sins. Jesus told Satan, *"No!"* He was going to do
God's will no matter what. Just like Jesus, you have power
over Satan too. Stand up to that voice that tells you to do
wrong. Say, "No!" When you keep saying, "No!" the devil
won't just walk away; he'll run!

• •

*Dear God, when I hear Satan's voice, help me
to stand strong and make him run away. Amen.*

THREE IN ONE

*"Baptize them in the name of the Father
and of the Son and of the Holy Spirit."*
MATTHEW 28:19

We don't know how He does it, but God has the amazing superpower of being three persons in one. God is the Father of the universe, ruler of everything. He is also Jesus, the world's Savior. And God is the Holy Spirit—that good and perfect Leader who speaks to your heart and guides you to do what is right.

• •

*Dear God, You are the only three-in-one
God and the only true God. Amen.*

AMAZING GOD

Trust in the Lord with all your heart, and
do not trust in your own understanding.
PROVERBS 3:5

There's so much about God we can't understand, like how He can be Father, Son, and Holy Spirit all at the same time. Or how God can be everywhere all at once or how He always knows everything, big and little, that's happening on earth. God is so much smarter than we are that we can't understand. We just have to trust in Him.

• •

Dear God, I trust in You and in Your love for me. Amen.

JOHN THE BAPTIST

*"For you will go before the Lord
to make the way ready for Him."*
LUKE 1:76

God knew even before Jesus was born who the special helpers would be in Jesus' life. One of them was Jesus' cousin John. Before John was born, God already had a plan for him. He would be the helper to tell people that Jesus was coming to save the world. When John grew up, he baptized people and told them to give up sin and do what was right.

● ●

*Dear God, thank You for providing helpers
for me throughout my life. Amen.*

DON'T JUDGE

"Do not judge, or you too will be judged."
MATTHEW 7:1 NIV

John the Baptist lived in the desert. He ate locusts—bugs that look like grasshoppers—and wild honey. His clothes were made from camels' hair. John came out of the desert shouting, "Turn back to God! The kingdom of heaven will soon be here" (Matthew 3:2 CEV). God used this loud, strange-looking man to do great work. We can learn from John that we shouldn't judge others by how they look and what they wear.

• •

*Dear God, teach me not to judge those
who look different from me. Amen.*

EVERYONE IS DIFFERENT

As much as you can, live in peace with all men.
ROMANS 12:18

The Bible is about all kinds of people—people who are different in so many ways. Some Bible stories show us how to get along with and live at peace with each other. When we put into action what we learn from the Bible, our love for God and others grows stronger all the time.

• •

Dear God, when I read the Bible, teach me how You want me to live and how to get along with others. Amen.

DIFFERENT AND SPECIAL

We are the clay, and You are our pot maker.
All of us are the work of Your hand.
ISAIAH 64:8

God is like an artist. He makes each person different.
That's how God made you, one of a kind and special. You are
His work of art. People are different in many ways: where
they come from, things they are good at, what they like
and don't like....What makes you feel special and one of
a kind?

● ●

Dear God, thank You for making each one
of us to be special and different. Amen.

GOD'S BIG FAMILY

The earth is the Lord's. . .and all who live in it.
PSALM 24:1

Everyone who receives Jesus as Savior is a member of God's family. It doesn't matter where you live. You are His. God put His people in different countries all over the world. It's fun finding out about people who live in other places. You can explore the world right where you are by watching videos and reading about how people in other countries live. Do you know someone who lives in a faraway place?

● ●

Dear God, thank You for friends near and far. Amen.

SPECIAL GIFTS

God has given each of you a gift. Use it to help each other.
1 PETER 4:10

God gives each person different things they are good at. Some kids are good at making things. Others are good at teaching younger siblings. All kids have special talents, like being good at sports, drawing, or making music. What are you good at? The Bible says the things you do well are gifts from God. You should use them to please Him and to help others.

• •

Dear God, teach me to use my gifts to please You. Amen.

GOD UNDERSTANDS

*There are many languages in the world. All of them
have meaning to the people who understand them.*
1 CORINTHIANS 14:10

People all over the world speak different languages. Maybe
you have heard someone speak a language you don't understand. Another great thing about God is that He understands
every word every person says. God knows and understands
everything! Would you like to learn different languages so
you can understand too? Do you know someone who could
teach you?

• •

*Dear God, learning a new language can lead to
making new friends. Show me how I can learn. Amen.*

NEW FRIENDS

There is a friend who stays nearer than a brother.
PROVERBS 18:24

As you get to know new friends, you'll discover all kinds
of wonderful things about them. You'll learn how you are
alike, and you'll discover some interesting differences too.
Those differences will help you discover new things about
the world and each other. Always be on the lookout for new
friends. You'll find them everywhere—at school, church, in
your neighborhood. . . And remember: you'll always have
one best Friend—Jesus!

*Dear God, new friends are everywhere.
Please help me to find them. Amen.*

EVERYONE IS BEAUTIFUL

*People, animals, birds, and fish are each
made of flesh, but none of them are alike.*
1 CORINTHIANS 15:39 CEV

When God created animals, He gave their fur different
colors and patterns. Zebras have stripes; leopards have
spots. Fish have scales in different colors—some are gray,
others are orange, white, blue, and red. God made birds
with feathers in almost every color you can imagine. And
when God made people, He gave them different skin colors.
Everything God made is beautiful.

• •

Dear God, I'm glad You made everyone different. Amen.

ANIMALS IN THE BIBLE

O Lord, You keep safe both man and animal.
PSALM 36:6

Even before God made people, He created the animals. Big sea animals and fish, birds, cattle, every kind of wild animal. When you read the Bible, you'll find all kinds of animals in there, even weasels, rats, geckos, chameleons, every kind of lizard, crocodiles. . . Some of God's animals still live on earth today, and others we can only imagine.

●●

Dear God, I'm amazed at Your creativity in making all different kinds of animals for us to enjoy. Thank You! Amen.

CROCODILES

"We cannot come near the All-powerful.
He is lifted high with power."
JOB 37:23

God has power over the animals and power over everything. He created His crocodiles to be amazingly strong with thick, fat legs; hard skin like armor; and big, sharp teeth. God said, "When he raises himself up, the powerful are afraid" (Job 41:25). People stay away from crocodiles. They would never wake one. Yet God has all power over crocodiles. He can make them lie down and obey like dogs.

• •

Dear God, You are more powerful than the
strongest animals. Nothing can stop You. Amen.

GENTLE GOD

*He will gather the lambs in His arms
and carry them close to His heart.*
ISAIAH 40:11

God is powerful, but He is gentle too. The Bible says Jesus is like a shepherd carrying little lambs in His arms. And it says God watches over the birds. Not one falls from the sky without God knowing (Matthew 10:29). God is gentle with you too. He watches over you and keeps you safe. If you close your eyes, you can imagine Him carrying you in His arms.

● ●

Dear God, You are so gentle and kind. I trust You. Amen.

IMAGINE

"Can you find out the deep things of God? Can you find out how far the All-powerful can go?"
JOB 11:7

Some animals in the Bible are a mystery. The Bible mentions their names, but these animals no longer exist. Or maybe they still live today, but we know them by different names. In the Bible, David says to God, "You broke the heads of the large dragons in the waters" (Psalm 74:13). Were they real dragons? A kind of sea monster? God only knows.

• •

Dear God, I like it that You make me use my imagination. Amen.

WHAT IS A COCKATRICE?

"The secret things belong to the Lord our God."
DEUTERONOMY 29:29

The King James Version of the Bible talks about an animal called a cockatrice. We have clues that it might have been some sort of poisonous snake, but we can't know for sure. We know it laid eggs like some snakes do, and it bit. Some Bible verses connect it with a flying, fiery serpent. Some things about God's creations are more than we can know.

• •

*Dear God, there are some things that You
know we haven't yet discovered. Amen.*

UNICORNS?

*He made the hearts of them all. And
He understands whatever they do.*
PSALM 33:15

We all know that unicorns don't really exist, right? Rainbow-colored, horse-like animals with a single horn on their forehead aren't real. But the King James Version of the Bible does talk about unicorns (Isaiah 34:7). We have clues. They were strong animals with horns. They hung out with bulls, both old and young. Whatever these Bible unicorns were, God made them. He understood them and everything they did.

●●●●●●●●●●●●●●●●●●●●●●●●●●●●●●●●●●●●●

*Dear God—dragons, flying snakes, unicorns! What other
strange animals did You create? I can only imagine. Amen.*

BALAAM

How great God is—God is more than we imagine.
JOB 36:26 CEV

Only God can make a donkey talk. A man named Balaam rode off on his donkey. God wanted to stop him, so He sent an angel that only the donkey could see. The donkey was afraid. It tried to get away. So Balaam beat the donkey, and God saw him do it. He made that donkey say, "What have I done to you?" (Numbers 22:28). Then Balaam saw the angel too, and he obeyed God.

● ●

God, You are so great. Nobody could ever
do the amazing things You do. Amen.

SOLOMON

*Solomon's wisdom was greater than the wisdom of all
the people of the east and all the wisdom of Egypt.*
1 KINGS 4:30

King Solomon was very wise. He understood many things
about life and shared what he knew. If you read the book
of Proverbs in your Bible, you will discover what Solomon
had to say. Solomon got his wisdom from the best Teacher
of all, God. If you read God's Word, the Bible, you can become wise too.

● ●

*Dear God, You are the best Teacher. I will
listen to and think about Your words. Amen.*

ASK FOR WISDOM

*You have now become a new person and are always learning
more about Christ. You are being made more like Christ.*
COLOSSIANS 3:10

You are learning new things every day. Learning in school
is important, and you can add wisdom to that. You become
wise by learning about Jesus and trying to become more
like Him. If you ask God for wisdom, He will help you to
ee the world like Jesus did. You will become wise about
what you do and say.

• •

Dear God, may I please have some of Your wisdom? Amen.

I WONDER

*The people were surprised and wondered
about His teaching. His words had power.*

LUKE 4:32

Are you curious? *Curious* is a word that means you wonder
about things. It's good to be curious, because that's how you
learn. You wonder. You search for answers. And then you
learn. People wondered about Jesus. His words were wise.
He had power to do amazing things. Are you curious to know
more about Jesus and everything in the Bible?

• •

*Dear God, the Bible is a big book. I'm curious about
everything that's in there. Please teach me. Amen.*

THE BIBLE

*All the Holy Writings are God-given and are made alive
by Him. Man is helped when he is taught God's Word.*
2 TIMOTHY 3:16

The Bible is called "God's Word" because everything in there
came from Him. Sometimes the words you read in the Bible
will have a special meaning to you. That's God speaking to
you and using the Bible to help you. The Bible holds the
answers to many of those things you wonder about.

● ●

*Dear God, the Bible is full of true stories and words
that teach and make me think. Thank You! Amen.*

A SECRET TOOLBOX

[The Bible] gives the man who belongs to God
everything he needs to work well for Him.
2 TIMOTHY 3:17

The Bible is like a secret toolbox. It's there for everyone who belongs to God. Whenever something in your life
needs fixing, you can pull out words from the Bible to
help. If you feel tired, angry, worried, sad, afraid, lonely,
or weak, the Bible will be your help. All you need to do is
memorize its words.

• •

Dear God, show me some of the Bible's tools
and teach me how to use them. Amen.

WHEN I'M WORRIED

*"Which of you can make himself
a little taller by worrying?"*
MATTHEW 6:27

Memorizing Bible verses will help make you strong. Here is one you can memorize for when you feel worried: "The name of the Lord is a strong tower. The man who does what is right runs into it and is safe" (Proverbs 18:10). When worry gets in your way, imagine God in His perfectly strong tower and you running into it. Worry doesn't exist there because God is inside.

• •

*Dear God, thank You for this Bible
verse and others that help. Amen.*

IF I FEEL WEAK

Even young people get tired, then stumble and fall.
ISAIAH 40:30 CEV

Have you felt something was so much bigger than you that you were too weak to handle it? Everyone feels that way sometimes. When you memorize this verse, imagine that you are strong like an eagle: "They who wait upon the Lord will get new strength. They will rise up with wings like eagles. They will run and not get tired. They will walk and not become weak" (Isaiah 40:31).

• •

*Dear God, when I'm weak, You'll lift
me up and make me strong. Amen.*

I'M ANGRY!

*Never pay back someone for the bad he has done to you.
Let the anger of God take care of the other person.*
ROMANS 12:19

The following memory verse from King Solomon will remind you that anger can turn into something huge: "Anger causes trouble and a bad temper is like a flood" (Proverbs 27:4). Instead of staying angry or wanting to turn your anger onto someone, give it to God. Let Him handle the anger for you.

• •

*Dear God, each day I'm adding memory tools to my
Bible toolbox. Thank You for teaching me. Amen.*

SAD

You have stored my tears in your
bottle and counted each of them.
PSALM 56:8 CEV

God knows when you cry. The Bible says He counts each of your tears and puts them in a bottle. Here's a verse to remember: "You have turned my sorrow into joyful dancing. No longer am I sad" (Psalm 30:11 CEV). Can you imagine dancing with Jesus? When sadness comes your way, talk with Him. Ask Him to replace your sadness with joy.

• •

Dear Jesus, You comfort me and dry my tears.
Your love and friendship bring me joy. Amen.

BEDTIME

I will lie down and sleep in peace.
O Lord, You alone keep me safe.
PSALM 4:8

There you are in bed not able to sleep. Here's a Bible verse to think about when sleep seems far away: "He lets me rest in fields of green grass. He leads me beside the quiet waters" (Psalm 23:2). Whenever you can't sleep, remember that Jesus is watching over you. So lie down in that grassy green field by the quiet water and get some rest.

•••••••••••••••••••••••••••••••••••

Dear Jesus, I will fall asleep feeling happy
*and safe because You watch over me. **Amen**.*

NEVER ALONE

Come close to God and He will come close to you.

JAMES 4:8

Do you feel lonely sometimes when your parents are busy? You are never alone, for God is always with you. The Bible says God holds your hand. This is the verse to remember for when you feel alone: "For I am the Lord your God Who holds your right hand, and Who says to you, 'Do not be afraid. I will help you'" (Isaiah 41:13).

• •

Dear God, when my family is busy, I sometimes feel alone. But You are always with me. Amen.

ANGELS!

For God did not give us a spirit of fear. He gave us a spirit of power and of love and of a good mind.
2 TIMOTHY 1:7

When things get scary, God will send His army of angels to protect you. Here is the best memory verse for when you feel afraid: "For He will tell His angels to care for you and keep you in all your ways" (Psalm 91:11). Thinking about God's army of angels will help you to be brave.

• •

Dear God, wow! I have angels all around me keeping me safe? That's awesome! Amen.

GABRIEL

The angel said to him, "My name is Gabriel.
I stand near God. He sent me to talk to you."

LUKE 1:19

When you read the Bible, you'll discover that God sometimes uses angels to do His work. The angel Gabriel appeared to Daniel in a vision. Daniel said Gabriel looked like a man, but something about his presence caused Daniel to be filled with holy fear, and he fell facedown before him. Gabriel told Daniel secrets about what God would do in the future. Gabriel is just one of God's angels. He has many more.

•••

Dear God, thank You for sending Your angels
to bring Your people messages. Amen.

MICHAEL

Then there was war in heaven. Michael and
his angels fought against this dragon. This
animal and his angels fought back.
REVELATION 12:7

Michael is one of God's head angels. He is a helper to other angels, God's chief prince, and a protector of God's people. Michael is also a warrior angel. The Bible says he is like a military commander leading an army of angels to fight against evil. Angels like Michael are all around you, protecting you too.

• •

Dear God, thank You for Your strong and brave
angels who fight for us against evil. Amen.

LUCIFER

*"You have been cut down to the earth,
you who have made the nations weak!"*

ISAIAH 14:12

Did you know that Satan was once an angel? Lucifer became too proud of himself and tried to take God's place, so God had to throw him out of heaven. Lucifer's heart is filled with wickedness. He is the one who causes all the trouble on earth. But don't worry. God is still in control, and one day Satan will pay for all the bad things he has done.

● ●

God, You have power over everything. Amen.

ANGELS ALL AROUND

"Do you not think that I can pray to My Father?
At once He would send Me more than 70,000 angels."
MATTHEW 26:53

Before Jesus died, He said that if He asked, God would send more than seventy thousand angels to protect Him. But Jesus didn't ask for angels. He knew God had a greater plan. Although you can't see them, God's angels are all around you. And just like Jesus, you can ask God to send them to help you whenever you need them.

● ●

Dear God, whenever I need help,
please send Your angels. Amen.

ANGELS IN DISGUISE

Do not forget to be kind to strangers and let
them stay in your home. Some people have had
angels in their homes without knowing it.

HEBREWS 13:2

The Bible suggests you could meet a stranger sometime who is really an angel in disguise. What does that mean? It means be kind to everyone you meet, and do your best to treat them in ways that please God. You'll never know, but maybe you have shown kindness to an angel God sent your way.

• •

Dear God, help me to treat strangers with kindness
because I never know if they might be an angel. Amen.

GOD'S HELPERS

Show me Your ways, O Lord. Teach me Your paths.

PSALM 25:4

Have you seen a house being built? Big work-machines come and dig the foundation. Then builders, each with his or her own special job, arrive and begin building the house. God puts just the right people together to get the job done. God does the same for you. He brings people into your life who will teach you His ways and help you grow up.

• •

Dear God, I know some of Your helpers. They are pastors, my parents, and other grown-ups. Amen.

UNDER CONSTRUCTION

I am sure that God Who began the good
work in you will keep on working in you
until the day Jesus Christ comes again.
PHILIPPIANS 1:6

Like a house, road, or anything else being built, you are under construction. God is putting you together piece by piece, using the things you've learned about Him. And do you know what? He's going to keep working on you all the days of your life. God won't be done with you until you meet Him in heaven.

• •

Dear God, keep working on me.
I want to make You proud. Amen.

JOSIAH AGAIN

*Happy is the man who always fears the Lord, but he
who makes his heart hard will fall into trouble.*
PROVERBS 28:14

Do you remember the first story you read in this book
about Josiah, the boy-king? His father had been a mean
man, and Josiah didn't have a good example of how a king
should reign. His heart was hard toward God. But God
softened Josiah's heart—He made Josiah want to know
Him. When that happened, Josiah began working to
please God.

• •

*Dear God, You changed Josiah's heart, and
You can change mine. He saw how You loved
Him, and I see how You love me. Amen.*

YOUR HEART

Your heart should be holy and set apart for the Lord God.
1 PETER 3:15

When you invite God into your heart, you will want to work for and please Him. Josiah did that! In his country, he tore down all the false gods—objects people worshipped instead of the One true God. Josiah worked to build a temple for the real God. And he led his subjects to believe in the real God and worship Him. Good things happen when your heart is right with God.

•••

Dear God, is my heart right with You? I hope so. Amen.

A STRAIGHT PATH

Josiah did what is right in the eyes of the Lord. . . .
He did not turn aside to the right or to the left.

2 KINGS 22:2

Josiah ruled for thirty-one years. As a boy and as a man, he did what God said. He followed a straight path that always led to good. When Satan's voice whispered in his heart, *Take this path away from God*, Josiah didn't listen. Josiah grew up to be a good man—a man who loved and pleased God.

• •

Dear God, I want to be a good man like Josiah. Amen.

MORE TO LEARN

But Jesus said, "Let the little children
come to Me. Do not stop them."
MATTHEW 19:14

You have learned a lot about God, but there is so much
more to learn. Read your Bible and ask questions. Look for
answers. Add more memory verses to your Bible toolbox.
Remember that God will forgive you whenever you mess
up. He loves you. Jesus loves you. You are always welcome.
Talk with God all the time. Ask Him to lead you today and
every day.

•••

Here I am, God. What will You teach me today? Amen.

SCRIPTURE INDEX

BIBLE STORY MATCH!

This exciting, "2-games-in-1" Bible memory match is inspired by Old Testament and New Testament Bible story favorites. Deck one features cards with art from Old Testament stories including Noah's Ark, Baby Moses, The Parting of the Red Sea, Strong Man Samson, Jonah and the Whale, and Queen Esther. Deck two includes art from New Testament stories like Jesus Is Born, Fishers of Men, The Woman at the Well, Jesus Walks on Water, The Good Samaritan, The Empty Tomb, and many more!